Writing Our Truths: A Guide to Self-Publishing for BIPOC Writers

Tayler Simon

Published by Tayler Simon, 2024.

WRITING OUR TRUTHS: A GUIDE TO SELF-PUBLISHING FOR BIPOC WRITERS

First edition. January 9, 2024.

ISBN: 979-8224897964

Written by Tayler Simon.

Table of Contents

Introduction

Serendipitous stories can find you when you least expect them. I found mine one month into building a community bookstore, Liberation is Lit. I have been amplifying books and stories by marginalized authors through this platform since 2019, and in June of 2023, I quit my full-time job working as a social worker in a community nonprofit. I took a leap of faith by taking this operation offline and starting a bookstore with the mission to spark collective action for liberation and community building among readers and book lovers by promoting stories from intersectional experiences.

I was browsing the shelves of books in a local thrift store to see what gems I could find to add to my online collection when an older Black woman stopped me.

"You look like you have style. I never see women wear waistbeads on the outside of their clothes. That's a bold move. What do you think about this top?" She held out a top for me to see. It was a long-sleeved black sweater with silver chain tassels embellishing the top.

"You look like you're about to go to a Beyoncé concert. I love it!" She laughed heartily.

As we spoke more about Beyonce concerts and the books I was browsing, she said her name was Bev and asked if I was a writer. I told her I was (because I was and still am working really hard to fight imposter syndrome and not downplay my ability as a writer so I can proudly claim the title).

"One of my dreams has always been to write a book. I don't know anything about writing a book, but I want to prove I can. Would you be willing to help me?"

My throat seized in that moment. "I write mostly blog posts online. I'm unsure if I'm the best person to help you. I have zero experience writing books or self-publishing", I responded sheepishly.

"You look like you know what you're doing and sound very knowledgeable. I think I was meant to find and talk to you today. God's got a plan for this little book."

After she said that and we exchanged numbers, I knew at that moment I would be the person to help her, that we met there for that very reason. The way she believed in me so fiercely took me aback. She saw something in me I wasn't able to see in myself at the time. She became my first book-coaching client.

Through the four months we worked together, meeting every other week combing diligently through her drafts, we completed and self-published her book. We learned so much from each other, and in a way, we both found our voices. She became more than a book-coaching client as we shared meals (and the occasional glass of champagne) at her kitchen table or on her back patio beneath the windchimes. I saw in her a fierce determination as she was writing through an injured thumb and dedicating hours to the revisions I gave her. She wanted to change people's lives through her book, and that passion sparked something inside of me.

I knew I wanted to write a book one day, but I never considered self-publishing. I imagined my book writing career would start a little like this: I would keep writing blog posts for my personal blog (with such a low readership because it's hard enough nowadays to get people to follow them, but especially difficult if you don't tell people you have a blog), and one post would go viral. A few publishing companies would reach out to me, all wanting me to expand on my viral post and turn it into a book. A deal would fall into my lap, and I would live happily ever after in my writer's dreams.

I thought this was the story of many of the writers I admire: Roxanne Gay, Samantha Irby, Zeba Blay, adrienne maree brown, Luvvie Ajayi Jones. Wanting to live out this fantasy discredited all the years of work these creatives put into their craft, the consistency to grow their audiences, and the doors slammed in their face before they had their work taken seriously.

I admit I looked down on self-publishing at first. I didn't think this was for serious authors. I thought self-publishing was for those who had given up on relentlessly pursuing traditional publishing or were too lazy to go that route. I know seasoned writers always say that a pile of rejections is par for the course. You get hundreds of no's to get your yes finally. However, I have learned from the spirit of those who self-publish that they are saying yes to themselves. They believe so much in themselves and their dreams of writing that they don't wait for someone else to validate them and their story. They already know what they have to say matters and are willing to put even more work into sharing that with the world.

Ms. Bev taught me this: I have to believe in myself, that sometimes opportunities come along, and you have no choice but to believe in yourself. Three months after I met Ms. Bev, I would go on to self-publish my first book. I didn't feel the weight of this accomplishment at the time. Self-publishing is a big deal, and I thought it was just something I did; like a lot of other achievements in my life, I didn't feel like they were worthy of celebrating. I created something with the audacity and vulnerability to put it into the world. That, right there, is magic.

When Ms. Bev became my first book coaching client, I committed to helping others get their stories out into the world, especially those of us that oppression tried to silence. When I self-published my first book, I made a promise to myself to share my own story with others to help and heal. White supremacy, capitalism, and colonialism told me and my ancestors that we are better off living our lives in the shadows, or like people like to say, the margins. I believe living in the light is our own taste of liberation in the face of oppressive systems. Loving ourselves and loving each other despite those with power trying to erase our stories and make us small is our own taste of liberation.

I can attest that books have changed my life. I can't imagine if Toni Morrison never felt the need to write *Beloved.* Or if Zora Neale Hurston let racism stop her from writing *Their Eyes Were Watching God.* Or if Maya Angelou never dared to write *I Know Why the Caged Bird Sings.* There is a reason why storytelling has survived for millennia in all cultures, passed down through the generations. Stories are how we make sense of our world, of love and loss, and all the things that connect us as people. Stories are how we imagine new possibilities and hope for those who come after us. We could use a lot more creativity, connection, and imagination in such a divisive and hopeless world.

The publishing world continues to be one that is very white. A new subgenre of fiction that exposes the racist world of publishing has been on the rise (see the novels *The Other Black Girl* by Zakia Dalila Harris and *Yellowface* by R. F. Kuang). Traditional publishing, especially those of the Big Five (HarperCollins, Random House, Simon & Shuster, Hachette, and Macmillan), is responsible for so much of the gatekeeping in the types of books and stories we are exposed to. Many of these big-time publishing companies believe and invest in the myth that our stories and experiences as historically marginalized writers are not universal and, therefore, not profitable. This, in turn, sends the message that the experiences of white, cisgender, heterosexual people are the only stories we all relate to; stories we may feel like we have to force ourselves to fit within.

In 2019, Lee & Low conducted an updated study to measure the diversity in the publishing industry. They found that straight, white, non-disabled cis women dominate the industry. And, of course, many of these women are still controlled by the straight, white, non-disabled cis men at the highest ranks of these companies. These publishers are recreating the world they live in and see every day, blissfully unaware of the rest of our stories or refusing to see their "marketability."

This is not to say that traditional publishing isn't entirely inaccessible for marginalized authors. We have seen some fantastic titles championed by larger publishers and their imprints, as well as the mighty and essential work of smaller, independent presses. I celebrate any author who works with a publisher, big or small, to get their story into the world, and this remains a goal of mine to accomplish one day.

The purpose of *Writing Our Truths* is to empower aspiring Black, Indigenous, Authors of Color (but also queer, trans, and other marginalized authors) with the knowledge and tools to successfully self-publish their work. I chose to focus on BIPOC authors for this first book because that is the most salient of my experiences as a writer. I also choose to use the term BIPOC (as opposed to focusing exclusively on Black authors) because I believe our experiences with racism and white supremacy, although different in manifestation, are connected. I don't just believe in opening doors to publishing; I believe in dismantling the door of exclusivity in publishing. Publishing your book is possible. The world needs you to share your story. If you need that extra push to believe in yourself, like I needed, let me be that push for you. I believe in you and your story fiercely. Let's work together to make magic happen, publish this book, and find your Radical Readers!

Writing Our Truths is intended to be one of several series of books about harnessing storytelling's power to live vulnerably and radically and create the world we all would do better living in. I am on a mission to turn passionate writers and creatives into StoryJustice Authors. I want to help you go from story to movement. This first installment will serve as a general overview of how to get started in the world of self-publishing or create your own table instead of waiting for a seat at theirs. Fiction and nonfiction writers can find valuable tools within these pages.

I believe in storytellers and artists to bring people together and heal with their words. Our world has so much destruction, and I think love through creation is the antidote. This book is your sign to use your voice and speak up for good. You may not believe in your power now, but you have the power within you to make a difference. And I'm here to help you realize that power.

Chapter 1
Understanding Self-Publishing

The first book I self-published was a poetry collection called *Phases*. I put together and edited this book in two weeks (more on that in Chapter 2). I wanted to see firsthand how the self-publishing process worked. When I decided to self-publish the collection, I was terrified. I didn't think I was good enough to write creatively. But when I got over my fear– my fear of what other people would think about my skills or my content– I took a breath and just put it out there. I didn't think I was ready to self-publish, but then again, I never thought I would be prepared. But, a poetry collection worked well as the first book I published, and I have reached so many people who feel personally connected to my work.

I learned a lot from self-publishing my own book. I learned so much to help my book-coaching clients in the future. I definitely made mistakes and took note of the things I would want to do in the future. I want to share those things with you in this book as well. I want you all to know what I didn't know.

I know it is easy to fall for the trap that self-publishing is as simple as writing all you can, uploading your final draft to Amazon Kindle Direct Publishing (KDP), and selling your book. But there were many things I didn't even consider before deciding to self-publish. There were many things I didn't have in place that I was scrambling to get together because I felt in such a rush, and I missed steps or had to do over the things I didn't know (like trying to make the minimum page count). Throughout this book, I will go over the things that will help you prepare to self-publish a book in a way that looks professional and polished, as if a traditional press published your work. We will start with the basics of self-publishing.

What is Self-Publishing?

Self-publishing is the process of writing, publishing, and distributing your print book or ebook. Authors who decide to self-publish take on all the matters and tasks traditional publishers do, such as editing, formatting, designing a book cover, marketing, distribution, etc. With self-publishing, you get total creative freedom and flexibility to adapt and license your intellectual property. You also get a more significant monetary return on your time and passion investment.

Self-publishing has evolved immensely over the years with the rise of technology and decreased stigma attached to self-published authors. The number of platforms authors have to choose from to self-publish their work has increased. With the popularity of e-readers and ebooks, getting self-published digital books to readers is even more accessible. Social media platforms have made it easier for self-published authors to build their communities and fan bases to share their work. All of these advances in the field have made writing books possible for so many people who would have had more difficulty getting their work out in the past.

The Benefits of Self-Publishing

Creating Opportunity: Just because you decide to start with self-publishing doesn't mean that it is your only option for the future. Many traditional publishers have become more open to acquiring authors' work after self-publishing. E.L. James, the author of the Fifty Shades series, is a notable author who got her start through self-publishing (she became a commercial name; however, her books are not my cup of tea). When you work to position your book successfully and build your community of readers, traditional publishers have tangible evidence that your book will sell well within the market. You are paving your own path and opening your own doors through self-publishing.

Creative Choice: Self-publishing is a viable option if you are just starting your writing career, and there are options if you don't have much money for upfront costs. This makes it very accessible for BIPOC authors. However, I don't want you to think self-publishing has no expenses. It is possible to self-publish a book completely free, but you do so at the risk of lowering the quality of the product. You can choose the aspects you want to invest your money toward (or invest your time learning how to do it yourself effectively). The more professional tools you can use, the easier and more polished your book will be (more on tools in Chapter 2). You can choose who you want to work with and what energy you want to bring into your book.

Print on Demand: One of my favorite features of contemporary self-publishing is the ability to print on demand. With traditional publishing, a certain number of copies go to print at a time. If you do not sell all of those copies and your book goes out of print, an author has to buy those extra copies (to try to market and distribute on their own), but they can be stuck with hundreds or even thousands of copies of their book, with no additional support from the publishing company to market or distribute the books in the future. Print-on-demand is a sustainable way to control how many books are in circulation. We don't create additional unnecessary waste, which also is better for the environment.

Limitations of Self-Publishing

Self-publishing is more accessible to every voice than ever before. However, some limitations to the process are essential to keep in mind. You shouldn't let these discourage you!

Being your own publishing team: If you want to make a living selling books as a self-published author, you become an entrepreneur. That can be difficult to reckon with if you are an anti-capitalist like me who doesn't like the more unsavory parts of a business or if you can't afford the instability of working for yourself in this economy. You really have to work to market, distribute, and sell your book. With tremendous flexibility comes great responsibility. It can be stressful to wear so many hats, primarily if you work full-time, are caretaking, or just want to focus on the art of writing in general. If you're going to write this book for yourself without the pressure of becoming a bestseller or making a lot of sales, you don't have to worry about these roles so much.

Limited reach: Having the same reach as with a traditional publishing company is very difficult. They have access to local and large-chain bookstores through distribution. They have access to media outlets on larger scales to reach more potential readers. Reaching your ideal readers isn't impossible. Depending on your current influence, connections, and willingness to put in some work to get creative, you can reach larger markets or create a pipeline from self-published to traditionally published.

Navigating copyright: Your work is copyrighted as soon as you publish it; you do not have to pay to copyright your work. Most self-publishing platforms give you a template for copyright protection at the beginning of your book. Even though you have that protection, it can be daunting to find a lawyer to navigate copyright issues and piracy should a violation occur. And because it can be difficult for self-published authors to protect themselves from these violations, we unfortunately become easy targets, especially with the rise of Artificial Intelligence.

A Word of Caution Against Using AI

It can be tempting to quickly throw together a book to self-publish and sell on Amazon or wherever using AI. I advise against this. As an avid reader, I can tell when ChatGPT has written something. I'm going to question your intentions for "writing" the book. Solely using AI to write your book cheapens the self-publishing field. Why would someone read a book when they can get the same answers from Google?

Writing is an art. Readers want to connect to authors, stories, and information that is authentic. What sets books apart is the person who is writing the information. You have to put yourself in your books, and you can't do that if you copy and paste your entire text from ChatGPT. Many artists have spoken out against the use of AI to create art. In the book community specifically, there have been conversations about requiring authors to disclose how much of their book was written by AI and traditional publishers banning the use of AI-generated book cover designs (by the way, you *have* to disclose how much AI you use when you publish on Amazon KDP).

This doesn't mean you can't use AI to do anything with your books. Sometimes, using AI to start an outline for a topic can be helpful if you are having trouble organizing your thoughts. I just discovered the site ArtBreeder, which is really fun to use to physically represent what your book characters could look like when you are creating your character profiles for a novel. But this is using AI as a tool that helps you with your craft, not depending on AI to do the heavy lifting. AI can never replace your creativity or ability to educate on a topic or present your personal story.

Choosing a Self-Publishing Platform

There are several self-publishing platforms out there. The most significant things to consider when selecting a platform are upfront costs, royalty rates, how each platform will format your work when publishing, where they distribute, and if they want exclusive rights to your work (i.e., you are unable to publish the book anywhere else such as with the KDP Select program with Amazon). See the chart below to see where the most popular platforms align with these considerations.

Platform	Royalties	Other Considerations
Amazon Kindle Direct Publishing	70%	Can distribute outside of Amazon unless you choose KDP Select
IngramSpark	Depends where you sell	Most popular independent distributor
Barnes and Noble	55-70%	Have other promotional opportunities for authors
Draft2Digital	60%	Can get universal book links for ebooks
Apple Books	70%	Only appears on Apple products
Publish Drive	100%	Monthly subscription rate

*Amazon is the largest distributor of ebooks. This makes it the best tool for exposure for self-published authors. However, Amazon does use its low pricing for books to price out the competition for independent bookstores (such as Liberation is Lit). I did publish on Amazon, but I direct readers and supporters to other avenues to buy my book when possible.

All of the platforms I listed above have been the simplified self-publishing process. You could also choose to do EVERYTHING yourself regarding print books. You can reach out to presses and pay to have your book printed in hardcover or paperback. You can use different options to save money, but this is still a pretty significant cost upfront. However, this is an excellent option if you want that professional look.

My Self-Publishing Experience

I can speak on my experience using Draft2Digital to self-publish my first poetry collection. I ultimately went with this platform because it would be the most accessible and flexible. I wanted to use one platform to distribute to several bookstores outside of the Amazon storefront (because I have my own personal issues with Amazon as a bookseller). Draft2Digital provides a universal book link, which was a very appealing feature for me because I could just post one link for all distributors of my ebook and print book. However, I still have to use two links because I decided to publish my ebook on Amazon (just because Kindle is the most popular e-reader) since there are limitations to distributing to Amazon from Draft2Digital.

If you do a print preorder with Draft2Digital, you have to have your book cover to continue, and you cannot make free changes to your print book, even before the release date. You can submit an unfinished copy to Amazon up to one week before the release date. I was disappointed that my print book wouldn't be in retailers sooner than two weeks after being released for preorder. Consider that timeline if you decide to do a preorder sale (more on that in Chapter 6).

The part of Draft2Digital I was most disappointed by was the formatting tool, as it was minimal, and I couldn't format some of my poems like I wanted to. I had to manipulate my Google doc several times just to have some basic spacing. Even if I had my formatting perfectly on the file I uploaded, the formatting would change in the preview.

Overall, Draft2Digital was an excellent option to start. It was free to get started, and I could distribute to several platforms simultaneously. Draft2Digital is a good alternative to Amazon if you don't want to distribute through them and want your book available through Ingram, the most popular distribution company for independent bookstores. I wouldn't suggest this platform to publish poetry, but it is acceptable for any other type of prose.

———◆———

With the evolution of self-publishing, BIPOC writers and StoryJustice Authors can write and publish a book (and have it reach more Radical Readers) more efficiently than ever before. When traditional publishing makes slow progress as an equitable space for BIPOC writers and StoryJustice Authors, self-publishing becomes a space where we can create our own tables when there is no space for us at theirs. If you think self-publishing a book is an option for you, but you are still on the fence about whether your story is worth telling, I will tell you why the world needs your story in the next chapter.

Chapter 2
Why You Should Write Your Book

When I published my first book, I had so many doubts about myself. Am I a good enough writer to publish a poetry collection? What if no one likes my writing, and I get all bad reviews? What will my friends and family (and everyone I have ever met) say when I publish such a vulnerable part of my life? These thoughts came up for me at every step, from writing to after I hit publish. I questioned my abilities as I decided to write *Writing Our Truths* because that is what white supremacy has engrained in me. It's easy to give in to those fears and doubts. Resistance is using your voice despite the doubts if you are using it for good.

Self-doubts are very common among writers. I believe many artists, especially writers, suffer from imposter syndrome, as well as academics and educators. We spend a lot of time comparing ourselves to other artists or educators who get a lot of praise and recognition. In addition to imposter syndrome, the work of BIPOC writers and educators has an extra layer of scrutiny from both within and without their communities. We live in a society where we constantly receive messages that our work is not good enough. We are told we must be twice as good to get half the recognition. We feel pressure to be a good representation of our community, which often means hiding much of our stories to not air our dirty laundry to outsiders.

Then, there is the issue of representation. When you turn on the television and browse the popular bookstores, you can find plenty of stories that prominently feature white, cisgender, and heterosexual characters and experiences and perspectives. Our stories are relegated to particular sections in the back of the store or small featured displays for whatever history or heritage month is happening. It is as if we should only be able to see and celebrate our stories during certain times of the year or as side characters created for a protagonist's enlightenment.

How society treats our stories is discouraging. It teaches us that our voices, experiences, and stories don't matter, or at least they don't matter to the white, cisgender, heterosexual experience. I dared to question myself, "Why do I have the audacity to believe that what I have to say is important enough for people to listen?" I believed my perspective was insignificant for a long time and purposefully kept myself silent.

I hope you hear and listen when I say you NEED to tell your story. We should never silence ourselves when there is a story inside of us. I think too many people get into writing because they want to make a lot of money. I used to be one of those people. But I have discovered that it isn't about fame and celebrity; writing is about being radically vulnerable. It's about being brave enough to share yourself with others because we have all felt alone. And in sharing those parts of ourselves that we may feel are less than desirable, we connect with others in that way.

Setting Intentions for Your Book

Intentionally living life is how StoryJustice Authors can build their movement through their books. Some people with incredible stories may not know how to use that story to mobilize people toward change or healing. You can be a person who tells a story or a storyteller who connects to readers. What intentions do you want to set with your story? Do you want to:

- Create a space for others to connect through their similar experiences

- Contextualize an issue you are passionate about

- Teach someone about your experience that many people in the world may ignore

- Ignite others' healing journey by talking about your own

- Use your story to imagine a better future

Connect your story to purpose through intention. What do you want this story to do for you? What do you like this story to do for others? Your intentions will keep you grounded throughout the publishing process. They will be your compass when you feel lost.

Radical Vulnerability

When I first published my book, *Phases,* I was scared to death. I thought about writing it under a different name. There is something so freeing about anonymity, especially for a chronic people-pleaser. I thought I could still share my story with the same intention if people didn't know it was me. But then, at the last minute, I decided that if I were going to publish these poems, I would do it entirely as myself. Many of my poems talked about how I hid the shadow parts of myself behind a facade of perfection and unlearning that to live my truth in alignment. I would be a hypocrite if I published those poems under a pen name. I would still be hiding behind a facade of perfection.

As I was publishing my first book, the words *Radical Vulnerability* kept repeating in my head and my heart. When I looked it up, I saw many people defining it as vulnerability being a radical form of healing for individuals and the community. So much judgment and shame in our world drive us further into isolation and despair. Through Radical Vulnerability, we can find our way back to ourselves by acknowledging the parts we need to heal and find connection and empathy with others.

Radical Vulnerability is why you need to share your story, whether it's through fiction or nonfiction. You may have gone through something that made you feel so alone while it was happening. You may have once been ashamed to share how weak you felt. There may be relationship wounds you want to explore. I am here to tell you that someone out there needs to see how you made it to the other side. I can attest that the Radical Vulnerability of my own book opened the door to healing some relationships in my life. Can you imagine how powerful it could have been to see someone else make it to the other side while you were still going through it? Can you imagine how powerful it could be to get closure for complicated interactions? You can be that in someone else's story. You can be that for your own story.

Writing your story can be a way for you to heal. Publishing my poems has been an incredible healing tool for me. For so long, I felt like what I had to say was dumb, bad, or insignificant. Through writing, I get to heal the little girl who felt that way. Writing is a way to explore new resolutions to your experience or examine deep feelings about what has happened in your life.

Radical Vulnerability helped me get over imposter syndrome. I'm not trying to become the next famous Instagram poet selling out stadiums. I set out to prove something to myself more than anything: that I could stop hiding the real me and put work into the world that would speak to the people who feel or felt just like me. I set this intention when I began thinking about publishing, and this intention continues to be my grounding principle.

Establishing Credibility

For those not looking to write *that* kind of book, I still want to let you know that your book also matters! As I said, academics and educators go through imposter syndrome and question their abilities. White supremacy tells us that the knowledge BIPOC people hold is inferior.

In the same vein, there is a stigma around supporting BIPOC-owned businesses because society sees them as less reputable and of lesser quality.

Self-publishing your book can be a great way to position yourself as an expert on a topic or within your field. You have valuable information from a unique perspective to share with others that can influence how people think or do things. You can have a space to share all your embodied, ancestral, and learned knowledge. Many people are now using ebooks to help advance their missions and showcase their skills, which could be an option for you. You could even use the ebook as a free resource to bring new supporters to your venture. If you decide to publish print books, you could take them to conferences or speaking engagements (more in Chapters 5 and 6). The possibilities are endless.

However, plenty of books are out there spreading false information and false promises. I think exploiting people's lack of knowledge to make money off of them is unethical. This exploitation is not what *Writing Our Truths* is about. I want to empower StoryJustice Authors to harness their power for storytelling for good, not to inflict harm on others or be predatory.

Helping BIPOC writers self-publish their books and become StoryJustice Authors has become my passion. I have been fighting to elevate the books written by BIPOC and other marginalized authors for a long time. You can see that with the origins and mission of my bookstore, Liberation is Lit. The mission of my bookstore is why I decided to use this book to help BIPOC writers and aspiring authors by aligning with my mission in the best way I know how: through books. I initially thought I wanted to publish this book traditionally, but in self-publishing, I decided and committed to practice what I was preaching. I wanted to show a way to build your own table to invite others to and say yes to yourself.

I was in a 6-week coaching group for aspiring authors looking to publish traditionally. The group's facilitator was the publisher of a mid-size, mission-driven publishing company I love. In one session, I asked how authors decide whether to self-publish or publish traditionally. In their response, I know they were trying to give a balanced critique on both sides, but the way they talked about self-publishing was why I wanted to write this book in the first place. They spoke of the publishing company's rigorous screening process of choosing the books they want to publish, bragging that they will never accept any book.

This response took me aback. Of course, small mission-driven companies don't have the resources to accept every book proposal. However, for a company whose mission is to raise the volume of voices that matter, boasting about exclusivity feels like upholding the very barrier they claim to fight against. I know every book and every story doesn't align with their mission or catalog of other books. Still, this exclusivity mirrors the gatekeeping of larger traditional publishers discerning whose story gets told. With the proper guidance, you can self-publish a book just as well, if not better, than traditionally published books. You are the best person to tell your story.

I hope you now feel empowered to tell your story. Now that you know what you want to write about, it is time to write your story. This process can be daunting, but I hope to help you with some tips in the next chapter.

Chapter 3
Time to Write!

When people ask me how long it took me to write my first book (a poetry collection), I always say that's an interesting question. It took both two weeks and three years. My process included going through my old journals to find every poem I wrote. I didn't think I wrote that many because I never considered myself a poet; however, when I mined through the pages and combed through the entries, I found poetry in the most unlikely of places. I discovered almost 150 poems from those readthroughs. Not all of them went in the book, but I got the building blocks of three additional books from those poems.

Through this process, I learned that you should never sleep on what you already have written. In another session of that 6-week group coaching program for aspiring authors, one of the guest speakers spoke about how so much of the first draft of her book came from her old Facebook posts and text conversations. She found so much gold in the content she had already written.

As a writer, I never throw anything away. I have all my old journals, even the terrible ones from middle school filled with petty gossip and those from high school filled with angsty poetry. Reading back over your content, especially if you have been writing for a while, can inspire you to rework it into something new. You don't always have to get overwhelmed by starting from scratch. However, if you need to start from scratch, that's okay too! You can use this chapter to learn tips on finding inspiration, staying motivated, and some tools you can use to keep all your information organized.

What is book coaching?

By now, you have seen me refer to book coaches several times throughout this book. There are many different book coaches with different styles and services they offer, but generally, book coaches are an accountability partner for you during your writing process. As far as my book coaching practice, I provide the following services:

- Assistance with creating goals for your book, including creating your outline, sales goals, marketing, and how you want to use your book as a means to creating a larger movement

- Weekly or bi-weekly check-ins during the writing process to make sure you are meeting your writing goals and answer any questions if you get stuck

- Referrals to professional editors, book cover designers, illustrators (for children's books), and any other services needed for the book

- Access to a community of other writers for peer support and knowledge sharing

Start with an Outline

The first step you want to do during the writing process is to prepare your outline. This outline is the road map that will keep you on track to propose your information to your readers. Once you have brainstormed and researched all the information you want to include in your book, you can organize that information into an outline. You can experiment with an outlining process that works for you, whether that's diagrams like thought maps or bulleted lists.

For nonfiction books, the easiest way to organize your information is to break your main points into sections and break those points further down. Those sections can be content sections or chapters, and the more minor points you elaborate on could be sections within your chapters. Depending on how detailed your outline is, you can easily turn your bulleted lists into your book's content.

For fiction writers, the outlining process is a little bit more elaborate. You're not just organizing information but building a whole new world and creating (hopefully) fully fleshed-out characters, ensuring it all connects to the big picture or theme you want to convey to readers. How you organize your story is crucial (see the following section about story structures). It can be helpful to add things like character profiles to form your characters into realistic people and find visuals you can refer to when describing the setting of your world.

I have seen several tools writers use to organize their outlines. The Scrivner app seems to be very popular. I have not used this tool, but I have seen demos showing how other writers use the app to organize their outlines and all the supplemental materials they need to reference to write their books. If you don't want to pay for additional software, you can use a regular document to write your outline or a good, old-fashioned pen and paper. Just ensure you keep your work organized in one place where you can find it when you are ready to write.

Many writers can get caught up in outlining, especially for nonfiction work. This step can be overwhelming, and it can be tempting to give up during this phase. If you find yourself getting inundated with what to include in your book or how to organize your information in a way that makes sense to your readers, it could be helpful to consult a book coach to assist you with developmental editing (more on the different types of editing in Chapter 4).

Writing a Compelling Story

No matter if you are writing fiction or nonfiction, telling the story is imperative. How you frame your story or stories is how you will stand out to your readers and have your book stand out among others with similar content. Stories are how we can humanize concepts. As I said before, storytelling has always helped humans make sense of the world around us, so this is how you should frame your book.

For fiction writers, there are many frameworks you can use to plot your story. A story structure is like a formula you can follow that can guide the pacing of your story to keep readers interested. You may remember the classic story structure taught in schools: rising action, climax, falling action, and resolution. There have been several variations popularized over the years. You don't have to use a structure (white men have popularized the most common ones, which is a testament to power regarding who has authority). Still, it can be helpful to use as a tool to organize your story in a way that keeps readers interested.

You can also apply these story structures to memoirs, should you choose to tell one long cohesive story of your life. Memoirs take a point (or points) in your life to convey an overall message or meaning to readers. Memoirs are not just about telling the events in your life in order; these events all need to tie back into an overall theme or message. One way to organize the events in your life can be through one of these story structures. What events in your life have felt like a Hero's Journey? What events in your life have changed you into the person you are now?

Another way you can organize information for a memoir is in smaller essays. Each essay can have miniature versions of these plot structures. You are telling several stories, but they all have minor themes that feed into a more prominent, more general theme (for example, how you entered recovery, how you repaired a relationship with your mother, your self-love journey after trauma, etc.). All books should connect to an overarching theme.

Empowering Through Educational or Inspiring Content

For nonfiction writers, there aren't many formulas you can rely on to structure your book, but as I mentioned before, make sure you organize the information you want to share with readers in a way that makes sense to them. Sometimes, authors can fall for the trap of writing in a structure that makes sense to them but may not make sense to their readers once they try to take that information out of their heads and articulate it to others. You are writing this book for them, so you should always feel like you are talking to your Radical Readers (more on radical readers in Chapter 5). While writers would love their work to speak to every single person, we can't be that broad, or what we say won't reach who it needs to reach.

Once you determine who you are writing your book for, you can narrow down the content that applies to your ideal Radical Reader. For example, if you are writing a guide for students, information on class instruction or mentoring kids won't be necessary for them to read; therefore, you shouldn't include it in your book. Information that applies to your readers will provide them value, and they can connect to the material more. Provide context for new concepts and find ways to weave points into your overall message.

Another thing to remember is to ensure you aren't providing information overload. If you give too much at one time to your readers, they will become disconnected. If you find yourself overwhelmed with organizing the amount of information you want to share or find in your research, that is a good indicator that your reader will also be overwhelmed. If you need to split up information into multiple books, you can. It all doesn't have to go in your first book.

Telling Others' Stories

I want to interject with an important consideration when writing memoirs. A common question I get (and the major plot points of season four of the show *Queen Sugar*) is how you navigate relationships when writing about painful parts of your life in a memoir that includes telling others' stories. You can manage this dilemma in several ways:

1. Try your best to make sure you have a conversation with the person before you feature their story in your book. You don't necessarily have to ask for permission, as this is your story to tell, and they play a role, but you do want to be transparent. Hence, there are no surprises for them that can cause friction in your relationship (or any surprise defamation suits toward you).
2. You can change names to protect the identity of those you talk about. If any of your supporters are family members (as they will likely be for your first book, more on that in Chapter 6) who know the context of the situation or if your platform is more significant and people can deduce who you are talking about (e.g., an ex-spouse), changing the name still may not protect the person's identity.
3. Be sensitive to the parts of your story about the person, and try to speak from your perspective. You never want to assume their intentions without talking to them first.

Finding Time to Write

The most common question I get from writers or aspiring authors is: how do you find time to write? This is the age-old question for all writers.

How do we find time? How do we find motivation? How do we prevent procrastination? Life is all about balance; sometimes, we have plenty of time to write, and at other times, we might not have any time (or mental energy) to write.

No matter what anyone will tell you, the answers to these questions are not simple, and there is no one-size-fits-all solution to these problems. You have to figure out what works for you. What works one day may not work every day because life happens (and many of us may be more neurodivergent than we initially thought). As you grow and evolve as a writer, your process will change with you.

You should block time on your schedule to write. When you find free time to write, protect that time like any other appointment. Do you find your most creative time (or quiet time when no one bothers you) is first thing in the morning? Middle of the day? Late at night? Optimize this time to get your writing done. Sometimes, when you work best doesn't align with when you write best, so keep that in mind. I prefer to do things early in the day, but my best writing is later.

I also love to write with writing groups. That way, I have an event I am more likely to show up to and have other people to hold me accountable for limiting distractions.

I am a runner but not a sprinter; however, when it comes to writing, I can't emphasize enough how much I love sprints. Your sprints can be any time from 20 minutes to 3 hours. I like to do multiple 20-minute sprints with lots of breaks in between. Breaks are important!

Finding Motivation to Write

1. **Set goals.** I made a lofty goal of writing 1,500 words daily to complete this book. Did I meet the goal every day? Haha, absolutely not, but setting the goal helped me stay on track. You don't have to set a goal that high. You can start with 15 minutes a day. If you want to complete a project in a certain amount of time, work backward to set the goal. Make your goals realistic, but don't sell yourself short.

2. **Reward yourself when you meet goals.** Everyone loves (and deserves) a little treat! When you meet your writing goals, reward yourself. I bought gold star stickers to put on my calendar each day I meet my writing goals (because that works for adults, too). If you want something more tangible, you could put a dollar in a jar each time you meet your writing goals and use that money to buy something nice.

3. **Stay focused.** When you set time aside to write, minimize as many distractions as possible. Go somewhere quiet or put your headphones in (my favorite music to write to is K-Drama soundtracks or movie/TV instrumentals, and I have no idea why). Put your phone on Do Not Disturb (unfortunately, this does not prevent me from compulsively scrolling).

4. **Have visuals to inspire.** If you are writing a novel, you can have a mood board that conveys the vibes of the story, including possible settings and character descriptions (as I mentioned in the outline process). If you are writing a nonfiction book, you can create a vision board that encompasses the main elements you want to include or motivational quotes to keep you grounded or inspired.

You should never rush your art. Sometimes, we can feel pressure to produce the most we can to make money and satisfy the demand of those who may consume our art (and demand it at a rapid pace). Capitalism does not care about your art. As I was writing this book, my sister had to remind me to take my time, slow down, and enjoy the process of writing. Even if you are not writing "creatively," putting together words and articulating thoughts to share with others as a story is an art form. Don't let money rush your process; always stay true to your purpose.

❖

Having a plan is great, but some writers (like myself) are also discovery writers; finding where the story leads me is more fun than having a super detailed plan before writing. That doesn't mean I go in without a plan, but I like what I can discover about myself and the work. Even when I sat down to write this book, so many things came up for me that I wanted to add to my original outline and first draft.

Figuring out what you want to say to readers in your book is one of the hardest parts, but it can also be the most fun part of the process. Even with the tips outlined above, sometimes you need an accountability partner to help guide you through the process, whether it is your first time or if you have self-published work before. A book coach can help clarify your goals for your book, hold you accountable with your writing schedule, and be the person to bounce ideas off of when you get stuck. A book coach can help you plan every step before you get to the writing process. Even so, you can write one book, but it can completely change in the editing process, which we will talk more about this *crucial* step in the next chapter.

Chapter 4
Editing, Formatting, and Cover Design

In the story I mentioned at the end of Chapter 2, the facilitator of the writing group I was in for aspiring authors mentioned that one of the major indicators that they can tell a book is self-published when it lacks professional editing. They said that when they pick up a book that has been self-published, they can know if it is low quality.

I am guilty of being a snob in the past when it comes to self-publishing. I would cringe when I noticed things about a self-published book that needed to be more professional-looking. Things such as spacing, misspellings, other grammatical issues, and font that is too big or too small used to make me cringe a bit inside. These things distracted me from the quality of the content I was reading. I believed this writer was an amateur and judged the content harshly.

If you don't invest in anything, you should invest in hiring a professional editor. Additionally, your book cover is one of the first marketing strategies to sell your book, so you will need a professional-looking design, whether you hire someone to do it or design something yourself using software tools. Your editing, formatting, and book cover design are integral to your book marketing. You can write the best book ever, but if these things are not polished or refined, you will have difficulty getting readers to take your work seriously. You should never overlook these things; if you don't trust your ability to do them yourself, you should always seek a professional to help. If you decide to work with a book coach, they can help connect you to professional editing if you don't know where to find one.

The Importance of Editing and Proofreading

I can't stress enough how important it is to edit and proofread your book. If you don't have money to invest in your book, you could start by editing yourself, but it is challenging to catch all the mistakes in your writing. When you read your own work, your brain automatically fills in words you missed and autocorrects the words you misspell. You know what you are trying to say, so your brain fills in the blanks with what it knows to be the logical progression. Programs like Grammarly can help, but they may not always catch everything, and their clarity edits can sometimes do more harm than good.

Many people are not grammar experts (including myself). What do you know about comma splices and dangling participles (I don't know much about them either)? This is not to say you have to be a grammar expert to be a good writer or storyteller, but you need a good editor. You can write a good book, but you can write an even better book if you edit it for clarity and grammatical errors.

Editing is not just about ensuring the grammar is rock solid; it is also about clarity and ease for readers. Again, a concept or story may make sense in your head, but it may be muddled for readers to understand. Having another set of eyes can catch those errors you may not notice. I use Grammarly for my initial edits and proofreading, which greatly helps. Initially, I had the free version, which was helpful, but the premium version helped me tighten sentences even more for clarity.

Here is a cautionary tale about the lack of editing: Because of the size of my platform on Instagram, I often have authors reach out to me requesting book reviews. Once, I had an author reach out to me to review her book on healing from trauma. The book cover was beautiful, and I was interested in the topic, so I accepted it because it held so much promise. When I started that book, absolutely nothing made sense. The grammar was acceptable, but I felt like the book was a bunch of unhinged

Facebook rants. The concepts went way over my head without explanation, and I felt like they didn't connect.

I contacted her and politely told her I felt more comfortable giving her feedback privately instead of giving her a negative review in public. She was not receptive to the feedback at all, insinuating that maybe I wasn't smart enough to digest the content since all her psychology friends who supported her work understood it. I, too, have a degree in psychology, and much of what she was talking about was rooted in religion, not psychology. I tried to tell her that I only wanted to help, but she was super offended and essentially started harassing me with defensive messages until I had to block her.

The moral of that story is to be open to feedback during the editing process. Writing is such a vulnerable experience, and when we feel like people are attacking our work, we can feel like they are attacking us as people. This is why I try to approach feedback or mixed reviews with the utmost care when I am the one who is distributing it. However, we must separate our feelings from the feedback. When someone offers constructive criticism, they want your work to be better, and they aren't looking for ways to tear it down (although there *are* trolls out there; more on that in Chapter 8).

Types of Editing

1. Developmental Editing: Content or big picture editing that looks at plot holes or thematic issues
2. Copy Editing: Fixing mechanical issues like grammar, spelling, word tense, and inconsistencies
3. Line Editing: Fixing stylistic issues like flow and content
4. Proofreading: The final review for last-minute fixes

Something that can be helpful in the editing process is employing alpha, beta, and sensitivity readers to give feedback on the flow and readability. Alpha readers usually read through the rough draft before the editing process; however, many authors do not elect to get alpha readers, as they would be reading through a less polished draft. Beta readers are more popular as they read through the manuscript after revisions. Sensitivity readers give any cultural sensitivity feedback, such as if you are writing about an identity you do not hold (e.g., a straight person writing a queer character, a cisgender person writing a trans character, or a Christian writing a Muslim character). Alpha and beta readers tend to be unpaid volunteers; sensitivity readers often charge for their services since they are specialized. Employing these readers will allow you to correct any mistakes or improve the content before it goes to your final readers.

Where You Start May Not Be Where You End Up

I recently read an Advance Reader Copy (also called ARCs, more on that in Chapter 6) of the book *Family Lore* by one of my favorite authors, Elizabeth Acevedo (I highly recommend this incredible author), while listening to the final release of the audiobook. I found a sincere appreciation for the editing process when I read the ARC and listened to the audiobook. I became acutely aware of all the changes Acevedo made from the ARC to the final draft for publication. She changed words, inserted new sentences, struck paragraphs, and rearranged entire chapters. Elizabeth Acevedo has so much talent as a writer, but even she needed robust editing.

Perhaps this is what makes Acevedo so great. Toni Morrison once said, "I rewrite a lot, over and over again, so that it looks like I never did. I try to make it look like I never touched it, and that takes a lot of time and a lot of sweat." Great writers know how to turn feedback and revision into even greater writing. Your first draft is hardly ever your best draft. If you think your first draft is as good as it gets, you may be rushing through the process.

With a good editor and alpha/beta readers, you may have to make large-scale changes to your work. You *must* be okay with this. You want your book to be the most reader-friendly version it can be. You don't want to write a book that goes over a reader's head so much that they put down the book and give you a terrible review. An editor may suggest you delete a lot of what you have written or have you rearrange chapters.

However, if an editor wants you to change your book's entire tone or themes, this is a red flag. Your work may not look quite like you originally planned, but someone should never alter your work to the point where you don't recognize what you envisioned unless you guide that decision and transformation yourself. You set the direction you want to take with your story, and someone should never lead you to a different destination than you originally planned.

It's What's on the Inside That Counts

Formatting is a step many self-published authors forget. How your book looks on the inside affects the reading experience. If a book deviates too much from standard formatting, readers will notice. How your book is formatted should add to the elements of the content, not take away from them. For example, formatting poetry books is so much fun. How you space the lines or the shape of the blocks of text can add dimension to the poems to make the reading experience more enjoyable. Formatting informational nonfiction books can also be immersive. You can play around with conveying information in charts, tables, and bulleted lists and emphasize different points with headings, subheadings, bolding, and italics.

However, readers will judge the degree of professionalism if you have inconsistent formatting that isn't stylistic. Uneven spacing between lines or paragraphs, a font that looks weird, or the words on the page are too big or too small can all look unprofessional. You want to check your formatting in the editing process or use a tool to format your book. I like to use the Atticus app to format my manuscript before I upload it to a self-publishing platform. You can use it to type your manuscript or upload your document to use one of their formatting templates.

All formatting tools are not created the same. As I discussed in Chapter One, the formatting tools on each self-publishing platform can sometimes alter the final book's formatting. I compromised the formatting of some of my poems because the tool changed so much of the formatting I had already done, and it wasn't sophisticated enough for me to change it back in the tool. You should also be cautious when uploading your manuscript to these tools, as the file type will alter these changes. If you don't want the formatting tool in the self-publishing platform to transform your editing too much, upload the file in PDF or ePUB; however, if you upload a DOC or DOCX in Amazon, that tends to preserve the formatting the most. Fun fact: If you don't have a fancy formatting tool, you can format your manuscript how you want it to look in your word processor and save it as an ePUB file.

Another thing to remember is formatting for print books vs. ebooks vs. audiobooks. These don't have to look drastically different, but if you want to publish in all these formats, you want to ensure your book looks (or sounds) good in each format. For example, how you break up content in print books and ebooks can vary slightly because of how print books and ebooks divide pages. If dangling lines on the page bother you (they annoy me as a writer, but not so much as a reader), this may change between formats. The margins of each format may change your spacing or the way your charts and images appear on the page. Your trim size will also alter the formatting. When formatting your manuscript, set the page dimensions to match the trim size of the book you want printed.

Genre   **Standard Paperback Trim Sizes**
Fiction   6" x 9", 4.25" x 6.87" (pocketbook), 5.5" x 8.5
Nonfiction 5.5" x 8.5," 6" x 9," 7" x 10
Children's 7.5" x 7.5," 7" x 10," 10" x 8

Source: WHAT ARE THE STANDARD BOOK SIZES IN PUBLISHING?[1]

As for audiobooks, the most significant formatting considerations are how you want to convey visual aspects of your book auditorily (many people include supplemental PDFs for listeners) and if you directly address readers as "readers" or say "if you are reading this book" and want to read the language as "listeners" or "if you're listening to this audiobook." Consider what formats you want to release your book in from the beginning so you can keep these adjustments in mind during the formatting process.

Judging a Book by Its Cover

The cliche *Don't judge a book by its cover* is a saying for a reason. We can't help but judge books by their covers. Your book's cover is the frontline for your marketing. If a book does not look attractive, engaging, enjoyable, or sound/professional, readers are less likely to pick up or buy your book. Some studies have found that 80% of readers find interest in a book based on its cover (Source[2]). Your book cover is the first impression

---

1. https://blog.ironmarkusa.com/what-are-the-standard-book-sizes-in-publishing#_853ae90f0351324bd73ea615e6487517__4c761f170e016836ff84498202b99827__853ae90f0351324bd73ea615e6487517_text_43ec3e5dee6e706af7766fffea512721_Now_0bcef9c45bd8a48eda1b26eb0c61c869_2C_0bcef9c45bd8a48eda1b26eb0c61c869_20the_0bcef9c45bd8a48eda1b26eb0c61c869_20numbers_0bcef9c45bd8a48eda1b26eb0c61c869_20you_3590cb8af0bbb9e78c343b52b93773c9_ve_c0cb5f0fcf239ab3d9c1fcd31fff1efc_sizes_0bcef9c45bd8a48eda1b26eb0c61c869_20in_0bcef9c45bd8a48eda1b26eb0c61c869_20the_0bcef9c45bd8a48eda1b26eb0c61c869_20United_0bcef9c45bd8a48eda1b26eb0c61c869_20States.

to readers. You can see that from the pretty book covers featured on TikTok. Your book cover needs to help readers understand the tone of the book.

Things to consider for your cover:

- Your book's title

- How color choice, images, and fonts affect the mood of the reader

- Does your cover match your book's content?

That being said, you should not skimp on book cover design. Sometimes, book covers can be simple concepts that can be easy to create. I created my first book cover on Canva with lots of input from my friends and family. Be very cautious of using stock photos, as some are floating around everywhere on the internet, which can take away from the branding of your book. Don't choose a cover design that only you like, but something that would draw you as a reader. Many authors elect to have their author photo as the backdrop of their book cover. If you want something more complex, make sure you hire the help of a professional.

The best way to think of a concept for a book cover is to look at similar books written in your genre or topic. Researching similar books can give you a good idea of what direction you do– or don't– want to go in. From

---

2. https://paperravenbooks.com/

choose-book-cover/#_853ae90f0351324bd73ea615e6487517__4c761f170e016836ff84498202b

99827__853ae90f0351324bd73ea615e6487517_text_43ec3e5dee6e706af7766fffea512721_Som

e_0bcef9c45bd8a48eda1b26eb0c61c869_20studies_0bcef9c45bd8a48eda1b26eb0c61c869_20ha

ve_0bcef9c45bd8a48eda1b26eb0c61c869_20shown_0bcef9c45bd8a48eda1b26eb0c61c869_20t

hat_c0cb5f0fcf239ab3d9c1fcd31fff1efc_design_0bcef9c45bd8a48eda1b26eb0c61c869_20of_0bc

ef9c45bd8a48eda1b26eb0c61c869_20the_0bcef9c45bd8a48eda1b26eb0c61c869_20cover_0bcef

9c45bd8a48eda1b26eb0c61c869_20itself.

there, you can decide how to work with a designer. Designers can help guide you with all things branding for your cover. Book coaches often have connections to artists and designers specializing in book covers if you don't know where to find one.

Book Descriptions and Author Bios

When I self-published my first book, I was unprepared with an author bio and a description. I had a lot of difficulty writing a description of my poetry collection. Writing summaries was never my strongest skill in English class, but to summarize three years of feelings distilled into poems in a way that markets my book? The task felt impossible.

Two things that helped me write a great book description are looking at a book in the same genre with the same tone as mine and using it as a template to write my own. I went through the description, line by line, and customized it to my own book and experience as an author. For example, if the description's first line is a sentence with strong adjectives that describe the collection's main themes, I outlined the main themes of the poetry. I picked two strong adjectives that resonated with my poems (thanks to an online thesaurus).

Here is my book's description (this template will work best for poetry collections or memoirs):

A genuinely vulnerable and transformational debut poetry collection from an original voice.

Waxing and waning through the journey of self-discovery and self-love, seasoned blogger and activist Tayler Simon reveals the shadows and illumination explored in her personal journals since 2020. This collection contextualizes themes such as sensitivity as a burden, wrestling with depression and anxiety, suffering from perfectionism and projection, unlearning self-sacrifice, and questioning who you are. Feelings are always present, showing up in your mind, memories, body, and relationships. Are they your friend, foe, ally, or enabler? Will you choose to be a witness?

You can look at a book you enjoy that is similar to yours and see how they formatted their book's description. How many significant points did the description feature? How did it choose to talk about the characters? How much of the central conflict did it disclose? You want to give readers a general overview but just enough to leave them wanting to experience more. You may elect to hire a marketing professional, but you know how to talk about your book; just talk about it in a way that will have readers looking to read more. Again, your book description is another essential marketing tool for your book. It will make or break if a reader decides to read more.

As far as author bios, you can do the same thing as with your book descriptions by looking at your favorite author bios and using them as templates. The main thing to remember is to highlight the parts of yourself you want readers to know about you. What do you feel readers should know about you to help them understand your book? You can be as fun or professional as you want.

Some highlights you could include in your author bio:

- Where are you from?

- Who are your people (including pets)?

- What other hobbies do you like to do besides writing or whatever niche you are writing about?

- Your educational background

- Any accolades, awards, or achievements you have

Here is my author bio you can use as a template (you will see an updated bio at the end of this book):

Tayler Simon is a writer, book lover turned bookseller, social worker, and seeker of liberation for all. She comes from southern roots, raised by three generations of love warriors. Tayler wrote her first book in second grade but resisted calling herself a writer until she started her own blog in 2019 and contributed to numerous online publications works on anti-oppression. Through her books, she has made a commitment to radical vulnerability, curiosity, and connection.

Self-published authors can easily overlook details like editing, formatting, book cover design, descriptions, and author bios. These details seem so small compared to the feat that is writing (and selling) your book. However, these details will set your book apart from "lower quality" self-published books, especially those thrown together with AI. It can be overwhelming to think of these details if you are not a professional, but you can hire professionals to help you. A good quality book coach can also help you keep track of these things every step of the way.

Now that you have your writing process down and are editing and formatting your book, it is time to think about building your community so you have a dedicated audience ready to invest in your movement. The next chapter will discuss building your community as an author.

Chapter 5
Building Your Community

When it was time to release my book, I was in this in-between situation where I had an existing community of readers through my bookselling platform, but I wanted to create an author community from scratch. I didn't want my bookselling community to feel like I was prioritizing my book over other people's works. I tapped into this established community of readers interested in uplifting books written by BIPOC authors, but I only promoted my book like I was featuring any other book. Liberation is Lit continued to be a space to highlight the many works of BIPOC, queer, disabled, and women writers; I just happen to be one of them.

I am still trying to find my footing in building a community specifically for my ideal Radical Readers. Radical Readers are the people you know will connect to your book. They are the readers you will inspire to take action after they read your story. I wish I had done more work to build my community while I was still writing the book so I wouldn't have to try to create the community while also trying to promote my book. Sometimes, it feels like building the plane while trying to fly it. To garner interest, I try to do cross-promotion on my Liberation is Lit pages. Still, I wanted a separate space for readers to voluntarily migrate to if they wanted to follow my author journey and learn more about my work to help other StoryJustice Authors specifically. I currently don't have an email list specifically for my work as an author, but I have gained the skills of building and maintaining an email list with my bookstore, Liberation is Lit.

When you use your story to ignite movements, all your marketing amplifies that movement. Having a reader community before you release your book can make spreading your message much easier when it comes time to market your movement through your book. As I mentioned, trying to build the community while making an impact with your book can be difficult. This chapter is all about different strategies to build a community of people who will be excited to read your book when it is time to start (or create) your movement through your book.

Finding Your Voice and Building Your Platform

If you want to use social media to amplify your movement through your books, you must discover your author's voice. The easiest way to determine your style is to base it on what kind of books you write. Are you a fiction writer specializing in a particular genre, such as romance or science fiction? Then, the content you talk about can be about relationships or world-building. Are you a nonfiction writer who wrote a memoir? You could focus on inspirational content or any social cause related to your experience.

Self-published authors may fall for the trap of trying to appeal to everyone because they want the world to read their books. Because of this, they make their marketing content broad to try to appeal to all readers. The best strategy is to think of the person you know who would be your movement's biggest supporter and speak directly to them. You would be surprised who else might want to join when they find themselves in the person you are speaking to and who might feel validated that you are talking directly to them.

Finding your ideal Radical Readers depends on the goals you set out for your book. What are the central themes and messages? What is your genre and subgenre? You can then match these goals to what motivates your readers. Are your ideal Radical Readers those who want to be inspired? Are your perfect Radical Readers people who love fantasy and exploring new worlds? Tailor your content around these motivations. Thinking about these goals can help you pick keywords and meta descriptions later (more on that in Chapter 6).

Your content will determine what platform will best serve your movement's base. If you want to focus on your writing, you could put most of your energy into long-form content in the form of a blog on your author's website. If you want to do more educational content or behind the scenes of your writing, you could start a YouTube channel about your writing process. If you produce more short, entertaining, or inspirational content, you could do Facebook, Instagram, X (Twitter), or TikTok. If you focus on making professional connections and using your writing as an entrepreneur, you could use LinkedIn.

You are certainly more than welcome to use multiple platforms to combine any of these strategies to reach your ideal Radical Readers. You can also use your personal platform where you already have an audience of family and friends. Still, I would suggest creating something separate if you want to keep your personal life separate from your professional endeavors. I separated my pages to have my family and friends choose whether they wanted to opt into my book content (similarly when I split my author profile and work with my bookstore profile and work).

Connecting to Your Readers

Now that you have decided what kind of content you will use, we will review the pros and cons of each tool you have when connecting to your community. You can use these tools to amplify your movement, not just build your community (see Chapter 6).

Social Media

Pros

- Reach thousands of people through helpful content

- Fun to create content based on entertaining trends

- Build an intimate community with close relationships with select followers

Cons

- Algorithms are forever changing, making it difficult to reach your people

- Keeping up with trends can be exhausting

- They can always silence your voice (they can suspend your account at a moment's notice)

Email List or Substack

Pros

- A space where you can share a lot of valuable information

- The most reliable way to convert readers into supporters

- No one can take your list away from you (just make sure you have permission to email)

Cons

- Difficult to build a substantial email list

- Creating content to service an email list or Substack community can be time-consuming

- Having a platform to host your email list can be expensive

Ads

Pros

- Reach a large audience very quickly to connect to your ideal Radical Readers

- Basically the most guarenteed way to get exposure

- Having a marketing plan that includes ads will strengthen how people find you

Cons

- Can be expensive, especially if you have a limted budget for your book to begin with

- Facebook and Instagram can limit your ads if what you are marketing is overtly social justice-oriented

- Can be tricky to figure out metrics to reach your target audience, lest you get lost in the noise.

Review Sites

Pros

- Platforms like GoodReads and reviews on Amazon are how many people get social capital for people to read their books

- People rely on what other people think to influence whether they will buy a book themselves

Cons

- NEVER PAY FOR REVIEWS. Many people will do reviews for free (just don't harass reviewers)

● You can get inundated with negative reviews that will affect you more negatively than positively

What is Substack?

Substack is a hybrid of a blog and an email. You can write longer pieces related to your movement that are not part of your book, release excerpts from your book, or release guides of resources related to your movement. You can monetize this list and charge for subscriptions (but you can also have free subscription levels).

Don't Underestimate Connecting In-Person

I have made so many wonderful and meaningful connections with readers in person. Readers get a chance to meet the person behind the pages in a much more effective way than through social media screens. Connecting to readers in person is paramount. You can connect to your audience in myriad ways:

Author events. Hosting author events can be so much fun. You can connect with your local library or bookstore (ask if they can stock your book on their shelves while you're at it) to see if they would be willing to host you to do a live reading or book signing. Libraries and local bookstores usually love having local talent to showcase. You can also collaborate with other authors with similar work to magnify your reach.

Launch parties. You can host a launch party when you schedule your book for release. Launch parties are an excellent way to drum up excitement for your book, get some orders, and celebrate the impressive feat of publishing your book!

Conferences and markets. When you are self-published, you must be boots on the ground, including being your own bookseller. Going to conferences– especially ones for writers or readers, art fairs (yes, you are an artist/creator), and anything related to your movement– to set up shop to sell your book can be a great way to connect with Radical Readers looking to support local talent. Make sure you have a way to collect emails to start building your list or direct people to follow you on Substack!

Establishing your Radical Reader community is imperative. Your community is not only there to read your book; they can also be there for you to lift you up when you feel down as a writer (which will inevitably happen). They serve as a reminder of who you are doing this for. They are your anchor. When you have a loyal Radical Reader community, you can turn those readers into advocates for change (more on that in Chapter 7).

I am working to build my Radical Reader community every day. It has been a transition from cheering for other authors to cheering for myself. Cheering for yourself and promoting your work can be a tough thing to do, and I know it can be challenging for other BIPOC writers since so many of us have the "work twice as hard" mentality that serves to trick us into believing that perfection needs to be the default. Your community wants to see you win. I want to see you succeed.

Building the community is only half the battle for elevating your movement. There are ways to use these tools to market your message, which can differ from building an engaged community. Finding Radical Readers is only great if they feel connected to your message through your book.

Chapter 6
Launching and Marketing Your Book

I did not give my first book the fanfare it deserved. I talked about it to try to drum up presales, but I didn't celebrate the accomplishment as I should have. My community kept telling me how much of a big deal self-publishing my first book was, but I didn't believe them.

My book launch announcements kept coming from a place of fear. I kept harping on how much I feared no one would like my book and how scary it is to be so vulnerable. People don't want to buy a book whose author projects so much fear onto its success. I have learned from that lesson. Your marketing should reflect the trust you have in your work.

Marketing anything– whether it is my bookstore, Liberation is Lit, my book coaching services, or my own books– is the bane of my existence. I don't want to feel like I'm begging people to spend their hard-earned money (this also makes me terrible at fundraising, which I learned when I was working in the nonprofit world) because I hate when I feel like people are pressuring *me* to spend *my* money. Over time, I have had to redefine my relationship with marketing, first by redefining my relationship to money and being compensated for my labor (unlearning values-based exploitation, especially as a Black woman, from nonprofits continues to be hard for me), and second by redefining my definition of marketing as "begging people to spend money."

Over time, I began to look at talking about my work not as marketing but as sharing my passion to get others passionate about important causes. As you notice, throughout this book, I don't use the term marketing. To me, *marketing* has the connotation of making the sale as the only end goal. Yes, you want to make people aware of your book to sell it, but if you are mission-driven and use your story to ignite movements as a StoryJustice Author, the ultimate goal is change. Your book is a vehicle for a larger mission.

Creating a Plan

The best way to create a plan to spread your message is to establish your goals and reverse engineer how you will accomplish those goals. I foolishly thought I was above SMART (Specific, Measurable, Attainable, Realistic, Time-Sensitive) goals. I thought I could start and sustain a movement with vibes alone. Things had just been working out, but to see actual growth, I needed to have goals I could use to measure success and pivot if needed. I didn't know how to create a plan until I realized how the plan was all dependent on my goals. Here is a chart of questions you can ask yourself to guide your plan. Once you answer all these questions, you can put together your plan.

Questions to ask yourself

Who are you trying to get your books to? Romance lovers? Survivors? People in your field? What do they like? What are they looking for?

Who are you writing this book for? Students? Professionals? Advocates? How old are they?

Where are your ideal Radical Readers? Do they congregate on TikTok? Do they like to stay informed through their emails? Are they at Comic-Con? Do they go to your local coffee shop? What problems are your ideal Radical Readers searching for solutions to? What are they googling? What issues do they want to learn more about?

How many readers are you trying to reach? What do you want your impact to be?

Make a plan

Who: This will be your target audience. Create an avatar of your ideal Radical Reader.

What: This will determine the voice of all your messaging. Write to this person in all your messages. Use your avatar and create a conversation about how you will speak to them.

When and Where: This will help you determine the best channels to use as your platform, whether ads and posts on social media, email marketing, going to conferences, or hanging flyers in your local coffee shop (don't underestimate the power of an eye-catching flyer).

How: This will determine Search Engine Optimization (SEO). Using keywords based on what your community is looking for is how readers can find your work in organic searches on Google, Amazon, or social media.

Goals: This is how you measure your impact from your plan to determine if your messaging is successful. Your plan is only as strong as your goals. Make sure your goals are SMART.

Example plan for my first book, *Phases: Poems*

Target Audience: Poetry lovers on a journey of self-love and self-discovery, especially Black women.

Author voice: Appeal to Black Women readers ages 25-40 who are interested in self-love and self-development

Marketing Channels: Social media (only posts for now), especially #Bookstagram and Instagram Poets, Email marketing to readers a part of bookstore marketing, and Black Writers Conference, as well as other creator markets that cater to Black women.

SEO Keywords: poetry for self-love, inspiring poetry, poetry for women, self-discovery journey

Goals: Sell 500 books within one year of the book's release. Get Reviews from 10 readers within the first three months. Build a community of 1,000 other writers and poets on social media by the end of the following calendar year.

Planning Your Book Launch

Your book launch happens way before your book's release date. You see movie trailers way before the actual premiere in theaters, right? Similarly, you have to work to drum up excitement for your book. Presales can be crucial for your book. Having your book rank on different lists like GoodReads and Amazon before your book even releases is essential to establish credibility and get it in front of as many of your ideal Radical Readers as possible. Here are some strategies you can employ to get exposure for your book even before you set it to release:

Build a Launch Team. You can offer Advance Reader Copies, or ARCs, to reviewers to get reviews for your book even before release. Having these reviews can give you an excellent foundation to influence readers to buy your book when you set it to release. It can also drive readers to preorder your book, which helps you in listings and rankings to reach even more readers. You can also pay for services like Kirkus Reviews to review and feature your book, but this service is exclusive.

Participate in a giveaway. Giveaways can be an excellent way to build your reader community while garnering excitement for your books or driving preorders. You can host one on your social media or email list, or GoodReads also has the option to host a giveaway, which can help you get your book on people's "Want to Read" list, helping you in their rankings and book suggestion algorithm (this is a service you pay for).

Offering extras for preorders. I have seen many authors offer extra goodies when readers preorder their books. These goodies can include gifts on theme with the book or story, exclusive author merch, or bundles with other books you have written. Offering incentives (if you can afford it) can encourage readers to order ahead of time and feel special for giving their support.

Cover reveals and book trailers. Like movies, you can create a book trailer for your upcoming release. Find visuals that match your book's aesthetic to create an engaging video. Cover reveals can also be fun to get people excited about your book launch. Visuals can engage people and make them want to learn more about your book.

After you get your plan together for presale, you can work on your strategy for your release date. How do you want to celebrate your book? You can do author signings or launch parties (see Chapter 5). I would also suggest celebrating yourself! Releasing your book is a huge accomplishment, and you deserve to celebrate yourself.

Other Ways to Market Your Book

When your book releases, you want to ensure you keep garnering as much attention for your book as possible because that is the crux of your movement. When creating your publishing budget initially, allocate money to market your book because this is one of the most essential expenses (aside from getting your editor). You can get your book in front of potential readers in several ways, both in traditional and untraditional ways.

- **Run ads on Amazon**: As most people choose the Amazon route for publishing, you can run Amazon ads that get your book at the top of the list. The best part of these ads is that you don't have to pay for the ads upfront; you will just pay a small fee every time someone clicks on the ad to get to your book.

- **Run Facebook, Instagram, or Pinterest ads**: I don't suggest investing too much into this method. Unless you are deep into self-publishing or writer Instagram, these ads won't appear on readers' feeds that often. However, if your goal is to build your reader community simultaneously, this could be a good option, especially through boosting your posts.

- **Run ads on other platforms**: There are numerous places readers frequent that you can pay for ads like GoodReads. As I mentioned before, you can also pay to host a giveaway on GoodReads, which is a way to get your book on readers' "Want To Read Shelves," a little continuous nudge to readers that your book exists and at one point they wanted to read it.

- **Sell your book in person**: As I mentioned in Chapter 5, you can go to different vendor events and writers' conferences to sell your book. Again, it is a great way to meet your readers face-to-face and have them get to know you as an author.

- **Find an unlimited source of your idea Radical Readers and connect to them**: Create partnerships with organizations that serve your ideal Radical Readers. For example, if your ideal readers are young people in the carceral system, see if you can do a program at a detention center or if your book can become a part of programs already existing in the detention centers to reach every participant.

- **Get to the media:** Find different opportunities to discuss your book and your movement on local news or during podcast interviews. You can also find opportunities to do guest posts on blogs as a way to direct people back to your book.

- **Pay for a blog/social media tour:** There are several companies that authors can pay to get their books to bloggers and influencers. As a part of my work promoting books, I work with two agencies– both owned by Black women– who conduct Instagram and TikTok tours: Bibliolifestyle and Cocoa Chapters.

Keywords and Meta Descriptions

Keywords and meta descriptions are essential to consider because they help readers discover your books. Keywords are common words or phrases readers might type in the search bar when looking for things they are interested in reading. What words or phrases might a person enter to find your book?

Meta Descriptions are how publishing platforms and distribution sites classify your book. This description includes all of the genres and subgenres. For example, if you are writing something fiction, is it for Young Adults? Is it Sci-Fi or Fantasy? If you are writing something nonfiction, is it a memoir? Does it include themes around recovery? Usually, you can pick up to 3 categories for meta descriptions, and every self-publishing platform will ask you for meta descriptions.

Self-published StoryJustice Authors must get creative when promoting their book and movement. You can't just post about it on your personal social media for friends and family to see or wish; it automatically ranks high on Amazon lists for your genre. Promotion has to be intentional, specific, and goal-oriented.

Promoting Your Book Beyond Release

Your presales went great. Your release day was fantastic. Now, what do you do? Don't stop talking about your books or your movement. You want to keep connecting to your community even beyond your release date.

Think back to your why and your intentions. Why did you want to write this book? What were your intentions? Your intentions can help you determine how you keep using and marketing your book years down the line. If you want to write this book to help people and change lives, keep helping people and changing lives (see more in Chapter 7). If you want to use your book to drive supporters to your mission-driven venture, keep promoting your book along with your passion. If you want to become a motivational speaker and transcribe your story into a book, keep finding opportunities to share your story and offer listeners a way to learn more about you and your story through your book.

Promoting your book is one of the most important things you can do to uplift your movement. Writing your book is essential, but you must get your work out to Radical Readers. Writing is hard, but being vulnerable and putting your work into the world can be even more difficult. It can be easy to let the process end after you finish your book, but you wrote it so you can change lives. You can't lose momentum because the work is still challenging you. You wrote your story because, as a BIPOC person, our stories have been silenced for way too long.

If you get stuck on any of these processes or need help, you can hire a book coach to help you create a solid plan. Book coaches can work with your strengths to find a way to connect with your ideal Radical Readers in a way that makes sense for your story, so your books don't go unread and your movement doesn't lose steam. Your story can take your movement to new heights.

Chapter 7
Creating Movements

Books have played an enormous role in changing my life. I have learned so much about myself and others by reading books written by people who live similar lives and those who live differently. Books and stories are why I started my bookstore, Liberation is Lit. I wanted to take what I was learning through these dynamic stories into making tangible change in my community and the world. And I also wanted to help others harness the power of books and stories. This is the movement I am committed to.

The stories that inspire us to change the world have to come from somewhere, and what better place to get those stories than for you to share your experience with the world? If you have a burning desire to share your testimony with the world to help others, a book could be a healing outlet for both you and your readers.

When I set out to self-publish my first poetry book, I wasn't out to change the world through my poetry. But my book has already done so much for people. I have people telling me that my poems complement their daily devotional. They tell me that they use my poems as affirmations. I am in awe at how I inspire others to go on their own self-love healing journeys. It's incredible to see this movement on both the reader's and the writer's sides.

Since publishing my first book, I became dedicated to another movement: Radical Vulnerability. As I mentioned in Chapter 2, we need more Radical Vulnerability worldwide. In such a divisive world where we are driven even further apart by capitalism and white supremacy, we need more ways to connect and help each other. We can create movements and change the world through this Radical Vulnerability with our stories.

Getting Intimate with Social Issues

Sociologists, social psychologists, anthropologists, and others study people and their movements. They study how they operate and interact and make informed assumptions and observations based on the patterns they see. Research can help us rationalize who we are as humans.

But there is a dark side to research. No matter how much researchers claim their processes are 100% objective, all people are complex and flawed, and they are the ones conducting research. Our perceptions shape our reality. So much of our science is rooted in racism, imperialism, colonialism, homophobia, ableism, and misogyny. Marginalized people are often erased from what is deemed "normal," and our existence is often pathologized. The data driven by numbers and statistics tell a limited story of how varied the human existence really is.

This is why storytelling and representation are essential to fill those gaps and create nuance in attempting to fit the human experience neatly in patterns, binaries, and predictable outcomes. Storytelling provides an opportunity to get intimate with social issues. We put faces and fleshed-out experiences into the data and the theories. We show how real the stakes are and how beautiful the possibilities are. Our lives are more than facts and figures.

Connection As a Form of Healing and Community Care

Our hyper-individualistic society has driven us to isolate ourselves more than ever, especially after the pandemic. We pride ourselves on pulling ourselves up by our bootstraps without relying on others; therefore, when we experience difficult times, it is hard to ask for help from others. We feel weak reaching out or admitting we can't overcome something alone. We feel isolated because we believe we are the only ones going through an issue, suffering in silence. On the flip side, when we think we are in times of prosperity, we hoard our resources (including knowledge sharing) and don't share with others who could be in need. Vulnerability works two ways: giving when we have the capacity and asking for help when we need assistance.

Through Radical Vulnerability and sharing our stories with others, we find that community support. We can lean on that community to validate our feelings, helping us to feel seen and supported. When we share our stories with others, we open ourselves up to empathy, increasing our ability to understand other people's struggles and connect them to our own. We focus on what links us as humans, how we experience joy and grief and love, instead of arbitrary (although with very real consequences) social distinctions that drive us further apart. When we show up as our whole selves to connect with others, we can show that we are not so different from each other. And when we see how we love the not-so-great parts of our stories out loud, we also give others permission to love and heal those parts.

But sharing our story isn't the only healing component. When we sit down to write our story, there is healing in that as well. When we start to craft our story, we can pinpoint pivotal moments that shape us into the person we are. We can examine our choices based on what was available to us at the time and what we have learned from these choices. We can forgive ourselves and potentially others in our lives, or at least understand them a little better. By learning more about ourselves, we can heal those wounds that may cause us to hurt other people.

This Book is More Than a Business

One of your goals for writing and self-publishing your book can absolutely be about making sustainable or additional income. I won't lie to you and say that one of my goals for writing and self-publishing isn't to make a living. I do want to curb your expectations and let you know that you will not get rich self-publishing or writing alone in general, not in the way mega (and pretty generic, in my opinion) authors do. And as much as I would like to be a radical anti-capitalist, you shouldn't feel bad for wanting to make money to be financially secure and make a better life for yourself or your family.

When you share a story that matters, one that is important to you, you have a unique opportunity to connect to people in a way more significant than making money. I know a lot of marketing professionals harp on the importance of sharing your story in your business to connect to customers. When you have this mindset of connection to make the sale, it can be easy to give up on your movement. You are seeking external validation, and when that doesn't come fast enough, it can be easy to abandon this vital work. Again, capitalism doesn't care about you making art.

When I started getting serious about writing, I wasn't interested in commodifying my artistic expression to sell my soul for the highest price. I was– and still am– much more interested in making people feel something, whether that's the pain of poking a wound they didn't know they had to heal it or the general joy that can come from just being alive. Making money and receiving praise for my art feels good, especially if it gives me the stability and flexibility to keep focusing on making more art for the world. The true reward I receive is the courage I gain as I put myself out there more and more and become okay with myself, even if everyone doesn't accept those parts of me.

It's Bigger Than You and Me

So much of business is rooted in competition. Writing is so different from that traditional mindset. Yes, we must make our story stand out to connect to the Radical Readers we want to connect to, but other writers are not our competition. Often, writing is overcoming the competition with ourselves.

With that being said, collaboration is going to take you much further than competition and isolation. Collaboration is the only strategy to truly build a movement. As I mentioned, when you collaborate with other writers, you can combine and expand your community. When you collaborate with organizations that are doing work that aligns with your values and your story, you can find new readers and more people to impact. Coming together as a community is how we can elevate our impact.

A myth they taught us in school about the Civil Rights Movement is that a handful of leaders carried the movements on their backs. While leaders like Martin Luther King Jr. and Malcolm X were so influential in organizing and influencing the masses, it was many leaders with boots on the ground and hands in the pot to make real change happen. When we let ego take over to make us think we should be the face of a movement, we set ourselves up for failure. We use our stories to be leaders in our own right, but we know movements are only as strong as the other leaders they create. King and X influenced a generation to find their own ways to be leaders within their communities, organizations, and families. We all have a role; one person can't do everything it takes to move the needle.

***

I believe in the power of individuals to create movements with their stories. I got into this work to organize storytellers in their own right. I am looking to build a movement with storytellers ready to get radically vulnerable to build empathy and connection while changing the world. I am not trying to be the leader of this movement, but I am looking to create leaders of different movements through Radical Vulnerability and storytelling.

Are you ready to use your story to build your movement? For too long, we have been told that our stories do not matter, but we know that they do by their impact on our lives. We are the ones we have been waiting for.

I know as much as we want to help people and use our stories to heal from within, we still need to take care of ourselves and use this process to learn and grow. In the next chapter, we will discuss how you can take care of yourself in this process and keep growing and developing as a StoryJustice Author.

Chapter 8
Evolving as an Author

When I started writing seriously, I thought I needed to come right out of the gate perfectly. I felt so bad about what I was coming up with, and I felt like my showing up and doing my best was never, and would never be, enough. It discouraged me from practicing and getting better at the craft. If I couldn't write something like *The Bluest Eye*, Toni Morrison's debut book, I would never be good enough to do anything (Toni Morrison took *years* to write *The Bluest Eye,* which was after she had been an editor for even longer).

After I released my first self-published book, I had similar doubts. I thought that what I put out wasn't good enough and that this would define me as an author for the rest of my days. I thought I had wasted my time putting my heart out there. Even if what I released was terrible, it wasn't a wasted time or opportunity to publish. I resolved myself to put out something even better next time. I learned from my mistakes and noted what I wanted to do better next time. Every time someone is drawn to my book, whenever someone says "mmm," I resolve to keep going. I know some people need my book to help them on their healing journeys. I know I have to keep on my own journey to keep creating to fulfill my intention for connection.

When you are an author, your first work may be bad, but there are things you can learn from the experience to make your next project even better. When you go in with arrogance to think that you know everything to make your book a bestseller, you are setting yourself up to make mistakes you could have easily fixed before publishing. This chapter will discuss how you can keep growing as a StoryJustice author on this life-long journey.

Be Open to Feedback

Earlier in this book, I talked about the author who asked me for a book review, but I decided to give private feedback instead. When I gave her the feedback and offered to work with her more, she insulted my intelligence and insisted that she knew best. She wasn't open to my feedback that the book was hard to follow and went over my head. I have never been met with such antagonism when I was trying to be helpful.

I know we writers can be sensitive about our ish (as the great Erykah Badu said). Still, when reviewers give the critique sincerely and constructively, we need to be open to feedback from readers and other writers. Taking this in can only make us better writers. I may not know your book the way you know it, but I know what makes me feel disconnected from your story.

However, as a word of caution, please don't get wrapped up exclusively dwelling on one- and two-starred reviews. That is fine if you don't want to read entirely negative reviews! Sometimes, reviewers can be trolls on any platform, and they just want a place to spew negativity, especially if that negativity is directed at the author as a person and not the work itself. Someone exposed a debut author in 2023 for spamming reviews on other books (predominately from BIPOC authors) from different accounts to make their book stand out over the other debuts.

Learn From Your Comps

Comps is short for comparative works, not competition. As I mentioned before, authors are not in competition with one another. However, if your comp is selling better than you or consistently making the top of the bestseller lists, see what you can learn from them. How are they writing their descriptions? What keywords are they using to rank higher in searches? How are their book covers designed? You can learn a lot from studying work that is similar to yours. Don't lose your authenticity by trying to be them, copy them, or steal their work.

Ask around if you are unsure how to do something or who to go to for different services. Build up your network of writer and reader friends, whether in real life or online. All of the writing communities I have been a part of have been so helpful in helping me navigate my process as a writer. If you ask, people are most likely open to helping.

If you feel overwhelmed by researching on your own or want to know what industry standards or trends are in your niche or genre, you can always hire a book coach. Part of my process as a book coach includes looking up your comps to give suggestions on how to design and market your book and working with you to make sure your voice stands out among the trends.

Never Stop Learning

As you grow and develop as a writer, you will learn new things about yourself and your process daily. I learned more about how to write more efficiently, edit my work better, and plan and outline my concepts. I also read up on improving my marketing skills and new ways to reach my ideal Radical Readers. I also learn so much from my book coaching clients because the best teachers learn from the students they are teaching.

You will never truly know everything there is to know about being the best writer. Writing is messy because it is an art rather than a science. The publishing world is constantly changing, as are reader preferences. You must learn all you can about the industry, your readers, and yourself as a writer. It's okay if you don't always resonate with something you wrote the same way as when you wrote it—our writing changes. We change and grow as people. We immortalized what we felt and where we were in the moment as our legacy, but we still can grow from that moment and look back fondly to who we were.

Overcoming Challenges

There will always be challenges you are up against as a writer, just like in the stories you share. You must remember that how you face and overcome those challenges is important. How can you turn those challenges into lessons to make you better?

Some of this is easier said than done. Sometimes, I can't find the inspiration, motivation, or time to write. Some days, I am my biggest critic and overthink everything I write (or ruminate over what I have already published). I let fear stop me from seeing how great I am as a writer.

Here are ten things that help me overcome challenges as a writer:

1. **Finding the best time to write**: I am most motivated at the start of the day, but I am the most creative at the end of the day. I try to write during these times of the day.
2. **Find your writing style:** Are you a sprinter? Writing in short 20-minute spurts keeps me focused and motivated more than just carving out an hour or so to write the whole time. Figure out what the maximum amount of time you can stay focused is.
3. **Stay curious:** Don't be afraid to explore writing in new genres or about new topics. Breaking out of your comfort zone can help you overcome writer's block or feeling stuck.
4. **Find a community of writer friends:** Friends and family really help motivate me when it comes to my writing, but no one keeps me accountable quite like my friends, who are also writers. They can help bounce ideas off of each other and just have fun writing together.

5. **Looking at other art:** Other artists and writers really inspire me to improve my own writing or art. I love looking at other media forms and reading many books.

6. **Keep a running list of ideas:** Some days, you don't know what to write about when writer's block sets in. I often have so many ideas that come like a funnel, or my brain wants to jump from idea to idea—keeping a list to return to the ideas I want to explore more helps.

7. **Just write:** Even when you don't feel particularly inspired or led to write anything for your project, just start writing something or free writing. You will be surprised what comes to you when you are just writing something personal for your eyes only.

8. **Revision is your friend:** Open yourself to constructive feedback and find ways you can improve your project. Many writers don't write well; they revise well.

9. **Take lots of breaks:** Sometimes, you need to step away from the project to gain clarity and direction or rest your brain. Breaks also help when you are feeling incredibly stagnant.

10. **Celebrate small wins:** I read one author rewards herself with an M&M every time she writes one hundred words and then gives herself a cookie when she makes her word count goal. Find ways to reward yourself.

We cannot fall into the trap of knowing everything as writers. We don't have to stay terrible if we feel like our writing is bad (although we tend to be harder on ourselves than we deserve), and there is always room to grow to become better, even if we are a best-selling author. If we are open to feedback, learn from our contemporaries, and commit to continuous learning, we can always be the best writers we can be.

One of my favorite things about being a writer is our ability to change and grow. We are artists, educators, and change-makers. The work we put into the world changes people and changes ourselves. I love that we never run out of things to say and new ideas to explore, create, and recreate. Evolution is in our DNA, so we all need to evolve as much as our work. Evolution is how we keep using our stories to move the world forward.

Conclusion

I immediately regretted publishing as soon as my release date came. I didn't want people to read my book because I felt like it wasn't good enough; I felt like I wasn't good enough. I kept thinking about putting my work into the world and having my loved ones and strangers see the parts of me I hid for so long.

It is easy for writers to feel like their work isn't good enough. We constantly compare ourselves to other writers or take rejection personally. I greatly doubt my greatness, but self-publishing forced me to believe in myself because I couldn't take the book back then. I opened the door, and there was no going back.

Self-publishing is a journey. You decided to achieve this significant accomplishment. You felt compelled and passionate enough to put your sweat and tears (hopefully no blood) into a project you wanted to share with the world. You did what you could to make it the best by investing in the editing process and the book's appearance. You put yourself out there to get your work in front of the readers you want to move with your story. You have the potential to start movements with just that story. How powerful is that?

People often tell People of Color that they have imposter syndrome. We are told that thinking we feel like we don't belong in spaces isn't a symptom of white supremacy. We see messages in our society time and time again that we don't belong and that our stories don't matter. A form of resistance to that pervasive message is that we don't belong. Our voices and stories and expertise matter.

I hope this book empowers you to start your own self-publishing journey. I hope you received the tools to feel more informed about building the most extensive movement possible. Remember, you are the one to define success for yourself. If you want to become a best-seller, establish yourself as a leader, or just publish a book to say you did it, that is a success. Don't let reviews, book sales, or following on social media define success for you.

Glossary

Self-publishing: the process of writing, publishing, and distributing your print book or ebook

StoryJustice Authors: writers who want to use their stories and books to mobilize readers to become part of movements for change

Radical Vulnerability: vulnerability as a radical form of healing for individuals and the community

Book Coach: an accountability partner for you during your writing process.

Movement: organizing supporters for a campaign centered around social issues in support of moving society toward liberation

Radical Readers: Readers you know will connect to your book and use your story to become a supporter of your larger movement

Writing/Writer Resources

Finding the right story structure for you[1]

Reedsy, hub for self-publishing[2]

Atticus, a formatting and writing tool[3]

Draft2Digital, a self-publishing platform[4]

Book Baby, a self-publising platform[5] (good for printing books and self-publsing children's books)

Substack[6]

Grammarly[7]

---

1. https://blog.reedsy.com/guide/story-structure/

2. https://blog.reedsy.com/

3. http://www.atticus.io

4. https://www.draft2digital.com/liberationislit

5. https://www.bookbaby.com/partner-referral/Liberation-is-Lit

6. https://substack.com/

7. https://app.grammarly.com/

Author's Note

Thank you so much for reading *Writing Our Truths: A Guide to Self-Publishing for BIPOC Writers*. I hope you have gained helpful insight and inspiration to turn your story into a movement. If you enjoyed this book, please consider leaving a review on Amazon and GoodReads. I am always open to feedback and would love to hear what you want to learn more about as I continue to write these guides.

If you are interested in my book coaching services, you can find more information on my website: https://liberationislit.com/pages/book-coaching. I would love to work with you!

Additionally, for transparency, some links to the resources in the Writing/Writer Resources page are affiliate links, and I may make a commission from any sales. This commission goes back to funding the bookstore Liberation is Lit.

Also by Tayler Simon

Phases: Poems
Writing Our Truths: A Guide to Self-Publishing for BIPOC Writers

Watch for more at taylersimon.wordpress.com.

About the Author

Tayler Simon is a writer, book lover turned bookseller, social worker, and seeker of liberation for all. She comes from southern roots, raised by three generations of love warriors. Tayler wrote her first book in second grade but resisted calling herself a writer until she started her own blog in 2019 and contributed to numerous online publications works on anti-oppression. Through her books, she has made a commitment to radical vulnerability, curiosity, and connection.

Read more at taylersimon.wordpress.com.